CANADIAN BRASS

Dixieland Classics

6 Jazz Masterpieces from the Dixieland Era

Recorded by The Canadian Brass

Arranged for Brass Quintet by Luther Henderson

3   BACK HOME IN INDIANA

12   GOIN' IN – AND MOVIN' ON OUT

25   MY MELANCHOLY BABY

35   ST. LOUIS BLUES

30   SUGAR BLUES

44   12TH STREET RAG

ISBN 978-1-61774-238-5

EXCLUSIVELY DISTRIBUTED BY

HAL•LEONARD® CORPORATION

7777 W. BLUEMOUND RD. P.O. BOX 13819 MILWAUKEE, WI 53213

www.canbrass.com
www.halleonard.com

LUTHER HENDERSON AND CANADIAN BRASS:
A Unique Legacy

Luther Henderson (1919–2003) was one of the major "behind-the-scenes" musical figures of the twentieth century, a master arranger who could give form, shape and richness to any melody. Rarely appreciated, the arranger's art is principally responsible for making America's professional-level repertoire of popular standards the envy of the world.

Henderson grew up in Harlem, and graduated from Juilliard at a time (1942) when the school had few African-American students. Soon after, he began a long relationship with Duke Ellington, writing many signature arrangements and symphonic treatments of the Ellington repertoire. In appreciation, Ellington called Henderson "my classical arm."

In 1958 Henderson made his Broadway debut as dance music arranger for the Rodgers and Hammerstein musical *Flower Drum Song*, and his Broadway work eventually encompassed 26 shows. He worked for decades as arranger on many prominent television programs. Shortly before his death, he was named a Jazz Master for the Arts by the National Endowment for the Arts.

THE CANADIAN BRASS CONNECTION

In 1978, RCA's prestigious Red Seal label ("Where Artists Become Legends") signed Canadian Brass to a long-term contract. Executive producer Jay David Saks had heard the Brass perform live on New York's classical station WQXR, and immediately set up a meeting with label head Thomas Z. Shepard. Just as the meeting concluded, Tom asked Chuck and Gene if Canadian Brass ever played the music of Fats Waller, and of course, received the instant reply, "He's one of our favourite composers!" The deal was made and the Brass set about recording *Mostly Fats: Ain't Misbehavin'*, the ensemble's premier album for RCA. When the Brass was still a few titles short of a full album, Tom called Luther Henderson (who had just completed RCA's Grammy Award-winning *Ain't Misbehavin'* cast album) and asked him to finish the album for the Brass. That phone call resulted in a key evolutionary step for brass music.

Luther Henderson created over 130 innovative works for Canadian Brass before his death in 2003. All these works have been published and are now being performed by musicians around the globe. Luther always maintained that his role as arranger was to accurately capture the spirit, emotion and even riffs intended by the original writers and performers. At the core of this impressive library are the jazz works represented here in this collection from the first quarter of the twentieth century.

Luther always tailored his music to show off the individual talents of the performers in front of him; this was also the approach he had taken when working with the Ellington band. Canadian Brass trumpeter Fred Mills virtually invented the role for piccolo trumpet within the brass quintet medium, and Luther took great advantage of this for his jazz writing, sometimes using the piccolo as a clarinet voice, sometimes as a lead trumpet, and often as a lyrical soprano voice. Canadian Brass horn players Marty Hackleman and David Ohanian opened Luther's ears to the incredible potential of the horn as a solo voice in jazz. Luther had been hugely impressed with Canadian Brass trumpeter Ron Romm, and penned many now-classic arrangements to feature his memorable talents; when recording these pieces on *High Society* it seemed a natural fit to invite Ron back to play, adding his own authoritative voice to this tribute to the master. Luther always relied on Gene Watts to assist "classical" musicians in interpreting his jazz realizations, and Chuck was not only Luther's musical bass (a key role), but his business base as well, as Chuck's publishing activities extended Luther's business interests around the globe.

Although Luther Henderson's music now belongs to the world, in a very real sense it was written "for" Canadian Brass.

Back Home In Indiana

James Hanley / Ballard Macdonald
Arranged by Luther Henderson

Music Copying by Tony Rickard, London, England

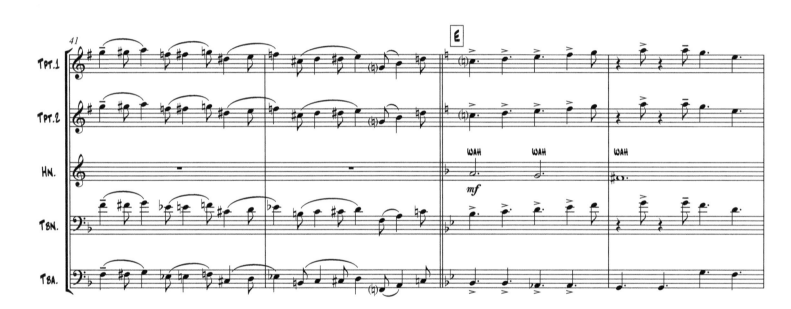

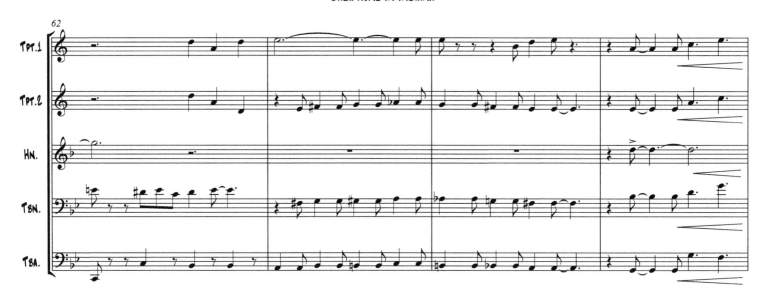

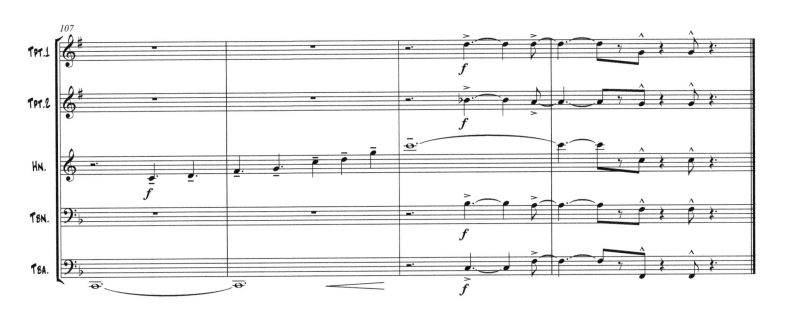

Canadian Brass - Henderson Legacy Jazz Series
Recorded on <u>Opening Day Recordings: ODR 9336</u>

Goin' In - And Movin' On Out

LUTHER HENDERSON

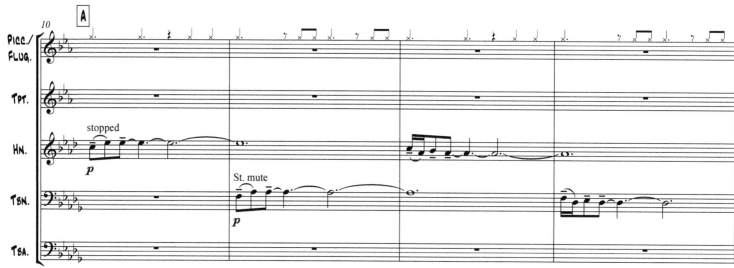

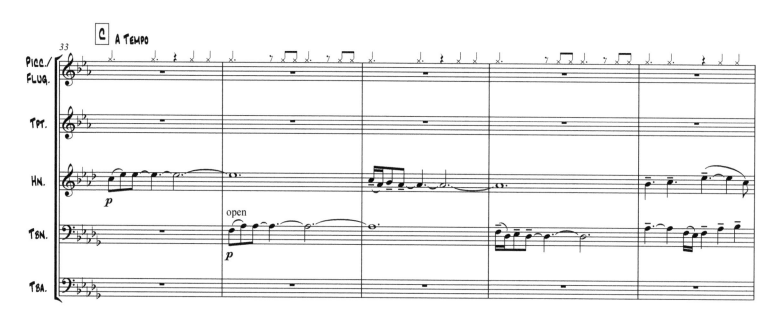

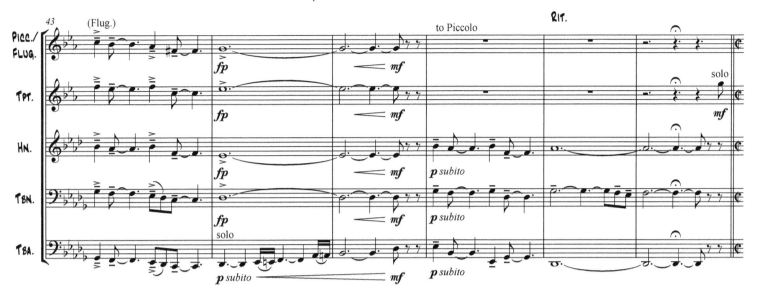

Part II — Movin' On Out

E **Allegro Moderato** ♩ = 108
Dixie Jazz Style

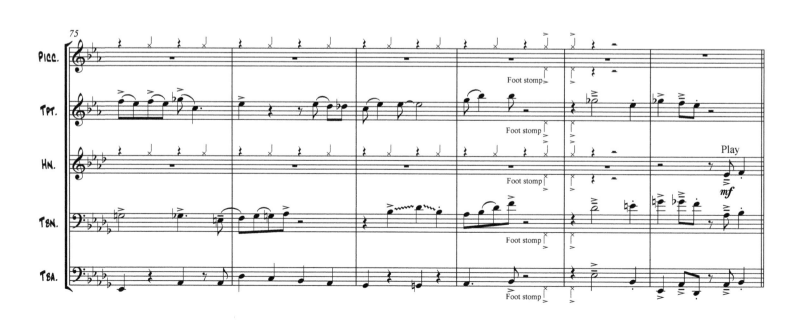

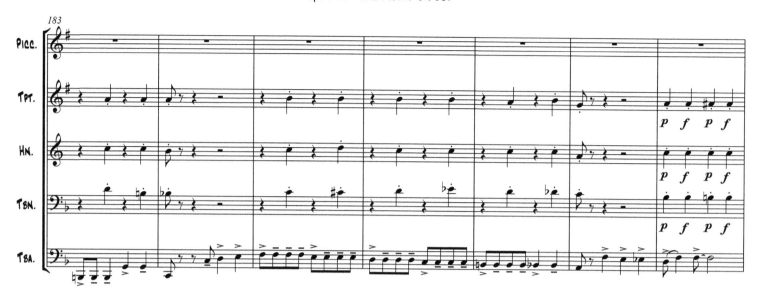

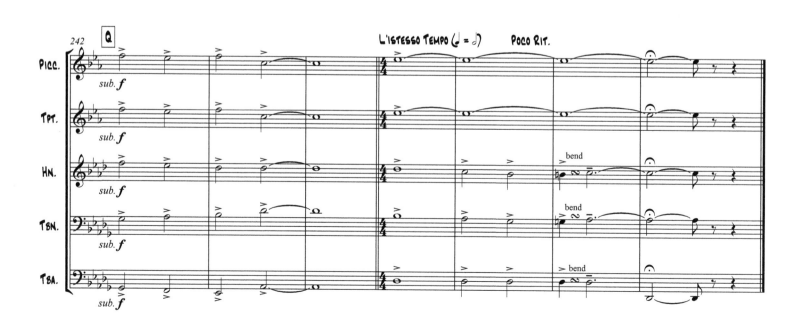

My Melancholy Baby

Ernie Burnett / George Norton
Arranged by Luther Henderson

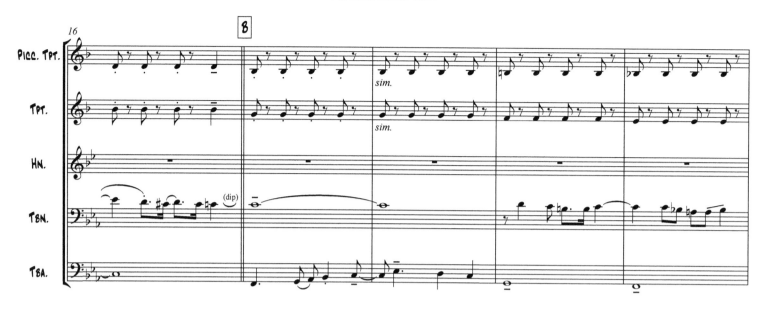

Canadian Brass - Henderson Legacy Jazz Series
Recorded on Opening Day Recordings: ODR 9336

SUGAR BLUES

Words and Music by Clarence Williams and Lucy Fletcher
Arranged by Luther Henderson

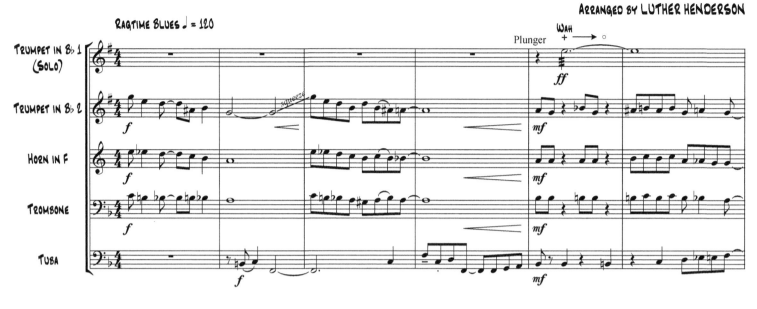

SUGAR BLUES

St. Louis Blues

W.C. Handy
Arranged by Luther Henderson

St. Louis Blues

Canadian Brass - Henderson Legacy Jazz Series
Recorded on Opening Day Recordings: ODR 9336

12th Street Rag

Euday Bowman
Arranged by Luther Henderson

12th Street Rag

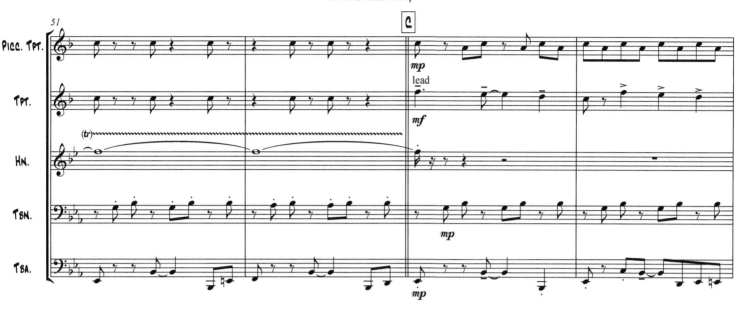